Helaman and the 2,000 Sons

written by Tiffany Thomas
illustrated by Nikki Casassa

CFI · An imprint of Cedar Fort, Inc. · Springville, Utah

HARD WORDS:
2,000, Helaman, alive

PARENT TIP: Practice the "silent e" rule in words with and without the e (cut/cute, mat/mate, bit/bite, rot/rote).

These are the good Lamanites.

They say they will not kill.

The bad Lamanites want to hurt the good Lamanites.

The Nephites help the
good Lamanites be safe.

The sons of the good
Lamanites want to help fight.

This is Helaman. He will lead
the sons of the good Lamanites.

There are
2,000 sons.

The 2,000 sons
help the
Nephites fight.

God helps the Nephites win.

The 2,000 sons are all still alive.
No one dies.

The good Lamanites are happy.

The end.

ISBN 13: 978-1-4621-4337-5

Published by CFI, an imprint of Cedar Fort, Inc. • 2373 W. 700 S., Suite 100, Springville, UT 84663
Distributed by Cedar Fort, Inc., www.cedarfort.com

Cover design and interior layout design by Shawnda T. Craig
Cover design © 2022 Cedar Fort, Inc.
Printed in China • Printed on acid-free paper
10 9 8 7 6 5 4 3 2 1